25 April 2014

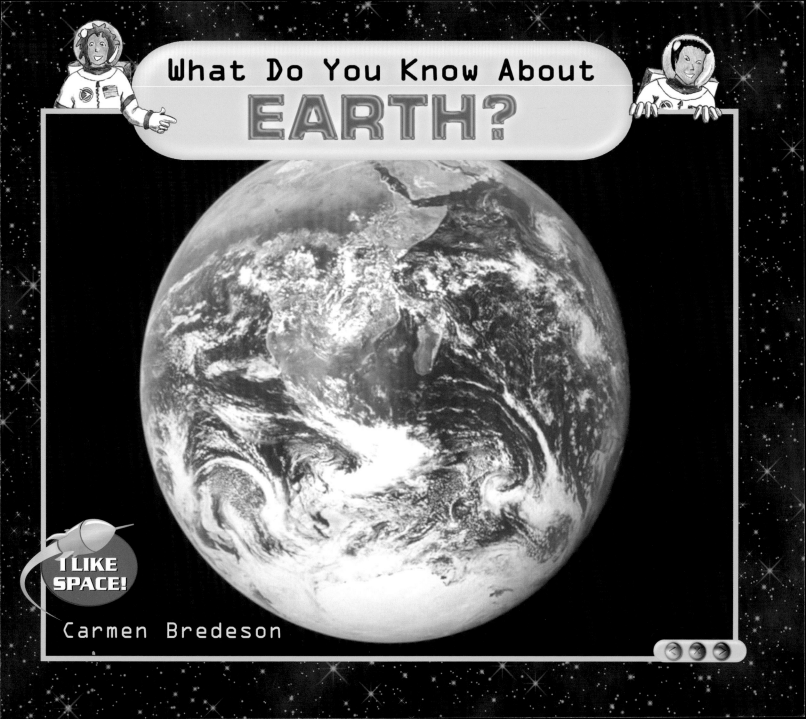

What Do You Know About EARTH?

I LIKE SPACE!

Carmen Bredeson

WORDS TO KNOW

atmosphere (AT muhs feer)
The air around Earth.

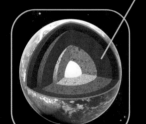

mantle (MAN tuhl)
The rocky middle layer of Earth.

orbit (OR bit)
To go around something else.

planet (PLA nit)
Any large, round world that orbits a star the way Earth orbits the Sun.

solar system (SOH lur sis tuhm)
A star and all the things that go around it, including planets, moons, and asteroids.

CONTENTS

What is Earth?

Earth is a planet that goes around the Sun.

If the Sun were farther away, Earth would freeze.

If the Sun were closer, Earth's oceans would boil.

Earth is in the right place for plants, animals, and people to live and grow.

Fun Fact

Earth is about four and a half billion years old.

How does Earth move?

Earth spins like a top. It takes a day for Earth to spin around once. While it spins, Earth also moves in a big circle around the Sun. It takes about 365 days (one year) for Earth to orbit the Sun one time.

Fun Fact

It is day on the side of Earth that faces the Sun. It is night on the side of Earth facing away from the Sun.

Earth spins
around this way
once a day.

Earth

Sun

Earth goes around the
Sun once a year.

What is the atmosphere?

The atmosphere is the air around Earth. It is made of gases, dust, and water. The atmosphere protects Earth from unsafe rays from space. It also helps keep Earth from getting too hot or too cold.

Moon

atmosphere

Earth

What is Earth made of?

The center of Earth is called the core. It is made of very hot metals. The next layer is the mantle. The mantle is made of both hard rock and melted rock. The outside of Earth is a crust of rock and dirt. We live on Earth's crust.

Fun Fact

Oceans cover most of Earth. Land covers only about one quarter of Earth.

inner
core

outer core

inner mantle

outer mantle

crust

What are earthquakes?

Earth's crust is not all one piece.
It is made of pieces, called plates, that fit
together like a giant jigsaw puzzle.
The plates rub and bump against each other.
The ground can crack and shake.
This can cause an earthquake.

edge of
plates

Earth Fact

Tsunamis (soo NAH meez) are
giant waves. They are caused by
earthquakes under the ocean.

What are volcanoes?

Gas and melted rock are under Earth's crust.
They heat up more and more. They push up
against the ground until it splits open.
Gas and rock blast out of the Earth.
Melted rock that runs out of a volcano is
called lava.

An astronaut in space took this photo of a volcano in Alaska.

Fun Fact

The islands of Hawaii were formed by volcanoes.

space rock

Earth

What made Earth's Moon?

melted rock

Moon

Scientists believe that long ago, a giant space rock crashed into Earth. Melted rock splashed far out in space. It made a ring that went around and around Earth. Part of the ring formed a ball that turned into the Moon.

Why is water important to Earth?

All living things need water.

Plants need water to grow.

People and animals need water to drink.

Earth is the only planet in our solar system that has so much water.

How are Earth's rivers made?

Rain or snow falls on the land. Water from rain and melted snow runs into streams. Many streams join together to make a small river. Many small rivers join together to make a big river.

Fun Fact

The Nile River in Africa is the longest river in the world. It is about 4,200 miles long.

What makes Earth's wind?

Sunshine warms the land and water.

The air above it also heats up.

This warm air goes up.

Cooler air slides into the place where the warm air was.

This happens over and over.

The moving air makes wind.

Earth Fact

A hurricane is a huge storm that forms over warm ocean water. Strong hurricane winds move around and around in a very large circle.

Clouds

Rain

Steam rises.

What makes Earth's rain and snow?

When water gets warm, it turns into steam.

The steam rises and cools off.

It forms drops of water on dust in the sky.

The drops grow bigger and heavier.

They fall back to Earth as rain and snow.

Ocean

What makes Earth's seasons?

Earth has four seasons.

They are winter, spring, summer, and fall.

Earth is tilted as it goes around the Sun.

North America is tilted *toward* the Sun in the summer.

North America is tilted *away* from the Sun in the winter.

It is summer in North America.

It is spring in North America.

It is winter in North America.

Earth's path around the Sun

It is fall in North America.

What is Earth Day?

Earth Day is celebrated on April 22 each year.
People remember how important it is to take
care of our planet. Some people clean up trash.
Others plant trees and flowers.
Many people take walks to look at the things
that make Earth beautiful.

Fun Fact

Earth has so much water, it looks blue from space. Earth is called the "blue planet."

Who studies Earth?

Geologists (jee AH loh jists)
study the rocks that make up Earth.

Marine biologists (muh REEN by AH loh jists)
study ocean animals.

Meteorologists (mee tee or AH loh jists)
study Earth's weather.

Seismologists (syz MAH loh jists)
study earthquakes.

Zoologists (zoh AH luh jists)
study animals.

LEARN MORE

Books

Birch, Robin. *Earth, Sun, and Moon*. Philadelphia: Chelsea Clubhouse Books, 2003.

Sanders, Nancy. *Earth Day*. New York: Children's Press, 2003.

Simon, Seymour. *Earth: Our Planet in Space*. New York: Simon & Schuster, 2003.

Web Sites

NASA. *For Kids Only: Earth Science Enterprise.*
<http://kids.earth.nasa.gov/>

NASA. *Space Place.*
<http://www.kidsastronomy.com>

U.S. Geological Survey. *Terra Web for Kids*.
<http://terraweb.wr.usgs.gov/kids/FunFacts.html>

INDEX

To Kate, our shining star

Enslow Elementary, an imprint of Enslow Publishers, Inc.

Enslow Elementary® is a registered trademark of Enslow Publishers, Inc.

Copyright © 2008 by Carmen Bredeson

Library of Congress Cataloging-in-Publication Data

Bredeson, Carmen.
  What do you know about earth? / Carmen Bredeson.
    p. cm. — (I like space!)
  Summary: "Introduces early readers to subjects about space in Q&A format"—Provided by publisher.
  Includes bibliographical references and index.
  ISBN-13: 978-0-7660-2945-3
  ISBN-10: 0-7660-2945-X
  1. Earth—Juvenile literature. I. Title.
  QB631.B74 2008
  525—dc22   2007002743

Printed in the United States of America

10 9 8 7 6 5 4 3 2 1

Every effort has been made to locate all copyright holders of material used in this book. If any errors or omissions have occurred, corrections will be made in future editions of this book.

Illustration Credits: Carl M. Feryok (astronauts); © 2007 by Stephen Rountree (www.rountreegraphics.com), pp. 16–17; Tom LaBaff, pp. 7, 23, 24.

Photo Credits: Courtesy NASA/JPL-Caltech, p. 2 (solar system); Gary Hincks/Photo Researchers, Inc., pp. 12–13; Image Science and Analysis Laboratory, NASA-Johnson Space Center. "The Gateway to Astronaut Photography of Earth," p. 5; J.N. Williams, International Space Station 13 Crew, NASA, p. 15; © 2007 Jupiterimages Corporation, pp. 19 (impala), 25 (insets); Lawrence Migdale/Photo Reseachers, Inc., p. 29; Mark Garlick/Photo Researchers, Inc., pp. 26–27; NASA Goddard Space Flight Center, p. 29 (Earth); NASA Marshall Space Flight Center, p. 9; Roger Harris/Photo Researchers, Inc., pp. 2 (core), 11; Shutterstock, blue starfield background and pp. 2 (atmosphere), 18–19 (background), 19 (cyclist), 21, 26 (beach), 27 (snow); U.S. Geological Survey, p. 12 (inset).

Cover Photo: Image Science and Analysis Laboratory, NASA-Johnson Space Center. "The Gateway to Astronaut Photography of Earth."

Series Literacy Consultant:
Allan A. De Fina, Ph.D.
Past President of the New Jersey Reading Association
Chairperson, Department of Literacy Education
New Jersey City University, Jersey City, NJ

Series Science Consultant:
Marianne J. Dyson
Former NASA Flight Controller
Science writer
www.mdyson.com

Enslow Elementary
an imprint of
Enslow Publishers, Inc.
40 Industrial Road
Box 398
Berkeley Heights, NJ 07922
USA

http://www.enslow.com